The history of the Zionist state

By Gregory Heary

For those who don't know how the conflict in Palestine started it is usually thought to have began in the late 1800s CE and gathered steam when Theodor Herzl published the Zionist book called "*The Jewish State*" in 1896 CE. Zionism is defined as the national movement of Jews and Jewish culture to establish an exclusively Jewish state. To be clear not every Jew is a Zionist and not every Zionist is a Jew. The first meeting of the World Zionist Conference took place in Basel, Switzerland in 1897 CE but Zionism existed long before then. In 1501 CE Christopher Columbus claimed to be the Messiah prophesied by the Calabrian Abbot Joachim. Columbus then began to call Christians to participate in a "last crusade" that was to be the climax of history before the end of time, but then he died. However before dying Christopher Columbus wrote a "Book of Prophecies" wherein he explained how all his discoveries perfectly fulfilled biblical prophecy and Columbus told the world what has to happen and what they must do so Jesus Christ pbuh can return. The prime religious prophecies/commands of Columbus were as follows:

1. Christianity must spread to every spot on earth and most of the masses must be converted to Christianity, one way or another.

2. The Garden of Eden still exists, is on earth and must be found.

3. The Holy Land must be taken from the Muslims and all Muslims must be removed from it, until that happens Jesus pbuh can't return to the Holy Land because Muslims are there.

4. An Emperor of the World must rule over everyone, this is necessary for the final Crusade to win the Holy Land and the Emperor will be the first to meet Jesus pbuh when he returns.

3

Despite Christopher Columbus claiming to be a Messiah and having written his "Book of Prophecies" over 500 years ago, many today actually fully agree with the above points numbered 1, 3 and to a lesser degree 4. Some Christians even want Columbus to be declared a saint. Yet oddly enough most people never learn this side of Columbus nor that he was a false a prophet who wrote a "Book of Prophecies". Most just get told he was a jolly genius explorer who discovered America for everyone, and if they are "honest" they'll admit he killed and enslaved a few natives. They don't teach the fun, dark, disturbing and exciting truth in schools. Schools even make it boring to learn about Columbus. Even when schoolteachers say Columbus was bad, they make him seem good because he was so much worse than what they know and they don't even know the half of nearly everything they teach. Soon after Christopher Columbus prophesied the holy land must be taken from Muslims for Jesus pbuh to come back the French/Jewish theologian Isaac La Peyrere taught in the 1600s CE that the Jewish Messiah would soon appear and join the French prince Henri de Bourbon to "liberate the Holy Land from the Muslims, rebuild the 2nd Temple, and establish a global government with the Jewish Messiah and French king as rulers". Peyrere influenced a Rabbi called Menasseh bin Israel who wrote a book called "Hope for Israel" which was published in Hebrew and Latin with the English version being published in London during 1652 CE. Menasseh bin Israel hoped for an eventual Jewish State in Palestine and thought the Jewish Messiah would be one of his descendants. The English ruler Oliver Cromwell agreed and decided to help Menasseh in his mission, first by allowing Jews to live in England so they could develop financially and cultivate a Jewish nationalistic pride/unity to serve them in the future for state-making. This was a

4

turning point in the Crusading era where the mentality shifted from "*Christians must rule the holy land at all costs*" to "*As long as Muslims don't rule the holy land it will be good.*" The next major advancement for zionism took place after rabi Yehuda Bibas preached Zionism throughout Europe in 1839 CE. One person who was influenced by this preaching was Colonel Charles Henry Churchill, the grandfather of the more famous Winston Churchill. In 1841 CE Charles Churchill wrote Sir Moses Montefiore, about his plan for creating a Jewish State:

"*I consider the object to be perfectly attainable. But, two things are indispensably necessary. Firstly, that the Jews will themselves take up the matter universally and unanimously. Secondly, that the European Powers will aid them in their views. It is for the Jews to make a commencement. Let the principal persons of their community place themselves at the head of the movement. Let them meet, concert and petition. In fact the agitation must be simultaneous throughout Europe. There is no Government which can possibly take offence at such public meetings. The result would be that you would conjure up a new element in Eastern diplomacy–an element which under such auspices as those of the wealthy and influential members of the Jewish community could not fail not only of attracting great attention and of exciting extraordinary interest, but also of producing great events. Were the resources which you all possess steadily directed towards the regeneration of Syria and Palestine, there cannot be a doubt but that, under the blessing of the Most High, those countries would amply repay the undertaking, and that you would end by obtaining the sovereignty of at least Palestine. Syria and Palestine, in a word, must be taken under European protection and governed in the sense and according to the spirit of European administration. I therefore would strenuously urge this subject upon your calm consideration, upon the consideration of those who, by their position and influence amongst you are most likely to take the* lead in such a glorious struggle for national existence. I had once intended to have addressed the Jews here in their Synagogue upon the subject, but I have reflected that such a proceeding might have awakened the jealousy of the local Government. I have, however, prepared a rough petition which will be signed by all the Jews here and in other parts of Syria, and which I shall then forward to you. Probably two or three months will elapse first. There are many considerations to be weighed and examined as the question develops itself-- but a "beginning" must be made--a resolution must be taken,"an agitation must be commenced", and where the stake is "Country and Home" where is the heart that will not leap and bound to the appeal? Supposing that you and your colleagues should at once and earnestly interest yourselves upon this important subject of the recovery of your ancient country, it appears to me (forming my opinions upon the present attitude of affairs in the Turkish Empire) that it could only be as subjects of the Porte that you could commence to regain a footing in Palestine. Your first object would be to interest the Five Great Powers in your views and to get them to advocate your view with the Sultan upon the clear understanding that the Jews, if permitted to colonise any part of Syria and Palestine, should be under the protection of the Great Powers, that they should have the internal regulation of their own affairs, that they should be exempt from military service (except on their own account as a measure of defence against the incursions of the Bedouin Arabs), and that they should only be called upon to pay a tribute to the Porte on the usual mode of taxation. I humbly venture to give my opinion upon a subject, which no doubt has already occupied your thought--and the bare mention of which, I know, makes every Jewish heart vibrate. The only question is - "when" and "how". The blessing of the Most High must be invoked on the endeavour. Political events seem to warrant the conclusion that the hour is nigh at hand when the Jewish people may *justly and with every reasonable prospect of success put their hands to the glorious work of National Regeneration."*

Coincidentally at the time Charles Churchill wrote this he was the British ambassador in Ottomon Palestine/Syria. Before Churchill's letter in 1841, The Bosnian Jewish Rabi Judah Alkalai proclaimed that the year 1840 CE was the "Year of Redemption", which was not a single year, but "a century, from this day until 1939", representing the "days of the Messiah". Alkalai taught that unless drastic powerful practical steps were taken, the opportunity for Jews to retake the Holy Land would be lost, and the next "year" lasting from 1940-2039 would be one of great hardship for everybody on earth since God will punish them unless Jews had ownership of the holy land. Rabi Alkalai joined the first Jewish Association for the Colonization of Palestine that was established in 1860 CE, in Frankfurt, Germany. Rabi Alkalai also attended the same Synagogue as Simon Herzl(the grandfather of Theodor Herzl) and they were close friends. Theodor Herzl was born in 1860 CE while Judah Alkalai moved to Palestine in 1874 and died in 1878 CE, so over the course of his first 14 years Theodor Herzl had many occasions to meet and talk with this Zionist rabi from 1860-1874 CE and it seems he really took to heart the Zionist dogma preached by Judah Alkalai since Herzl later preached it himself to greater effect. In 1854 CE the Ottomon State took out an interest loan of 16 million pounds from the Jewish House of Rothschild to pay for the Crimean war which it had entered due to it's alliance with Britain and France which led it to fight Russia on behalf of Napolean III. You see Napolean III claimed he wanted to destroy Eastern Orthodox Christianity as Russia sponsored and Nicholas I of Russia claimed he wanted to destroy Catholicism as France sponsored. The Crimean war was a religious war in other ways as well. France wanted

Catholics in Palestine to be treated better than Eastern Orthodox Christians were and Russia wanted Eastern Orthodox Christians to be treated better than the Catholics were. So both France and Russia wanted the Muslim Ottomons to favor one Christian group over the other, but Britain persuaded France it wasn't worth going to war over and then they both persuaded the Ottomon state that it should fight Russia to so as not to get "pushed around" by Russia. The Russian Emperor Nicholas I said that he didn't like the way Orthodox Christians were treated so he wanted to be in control of the Orthodox communities in Palestine and the rest of the Ottomon state so as to ensure they were treated as he saw fit. Nicholas I actually asked the Ottomon sultan in 1853 CE if he could be put in charge of Palestine, of course the Sultan said no and Russia said they would take control if it wasn't given to them. Naturally the Ottomons didn't like that attitude especially when it was coming from the same Russian Emperor who defeated the Ottomons in the war of 1828 CE. Britain and France said Russia had no right to demand such authority in Palestine, and they assured the Ottomons they would fight alongside them if they declared war against Russia; so they did and then went into debt as a result. Simultaneously and hypocritically Napolean III used financial and military pressure to be given proxy authority over the Christians in the Holy Land and attain preferential treatment for Catholics over Orthodox Christians and that's why Russia was so pissed and threatened war to begin with. Russia lost this war as well as some territory and fearing they would lose territory in America in the future they decided to sell Alaska to the United States in 1859 CE. Basically America got to buy Alaska because Russia lost the Crimean war to the Muslims and Russia feared losing Alaska to Britain in the future should Russia lose more wars against the Ottomons and their British and French allies. Russia soon fought the Ottomons again in 1877 CE but won and the Balkans became independent territories as a result. Due to the debt from the Crimean war and pressure from Britain and France the Ottomon state in 1856 CE promised equality in education, government appointments, and administration of justice to all regardless of creed; which contradicted Shariah law since an Islamic government can't be run by non-Muslim agents. But the Ottomons were in debt so they "modernized" with the western ways due to international peer pressure and financial pressure from the Jewish Rothschilds. Likewise the Edict of Gulhane proclaimed before the 1856 Paris peace treaty that ended the Crimean war abolished the Jizya for Christians living in the Ottomon empire and also allowed for non-Muslims to join the Ottomon army. Around this time religiously and governmentally speaking the Ottomon state stopped being a Khilafah ruling by Shariah law and became just a Muslim state since it was no longer applying the Islamic Shariah. Whereas this act by the Ottomons in 1856 CE was extremely innovative because Britain itself didn't allow Jews to be members of Parliament until 1858 CE, 2 years later, and even then they weren't allowed to advise the Queen. So the Ottomons in 1856 CE were more liberal towards religious minorities than Britain, despite Britain pushing the Ottomons to liberalize. In 1858 CE the Ottoman Land code was passed, due to a need to pay off debt, this allowed people of all religions to buy and sell land without the limitations that Shariah had previously imposed upon land transfers to non-Muslims. Thereupon many Jews took advantage of this to buy land specifically in Palestine. The law also required people to register their land titles with the state, which many people didn't do because to register meant you would have to serve in the military and pay taxes on it. In 1862 CE the German Rabi

Zvi Hirsch Kalischer published his book *Drishat Tzion* wherein he proposed a 4 point plan of action Jews could take to create a Jewish State in the Holy Land:

1. To collect money for this purpose from Jews in all countries
2. To buy and cultivate land in Israel(the holy land)
3. To found an agricultural school, either in Israel itself or France.
4. To form a Jewish military guard for the security of the colonies.

In 1869 CE the Ottomon Nationality law was passed, again due to pressure from Europe to "modernize", this law legally ensured identical treatment in Ottomon territory for all citizens regardless of their religion, which also contradicted Shariah. In 1873 CE the Ottomon Land Emancipation Act was passed and it decreed those lands that weren't registered were subsequently state property and up for sale so as to pay off the government debt that it owed to the Jewish Rothschild bankers from the Crimean war against Russia that took place 20 years before. On that note it is ironic that Russia also became indebted due to the Russo-Turkish war from 1877-1878 and Germany refused to pay Russian debts so Russia turned to France for financial aid and became allies with France while the Ottomons were struggling to make the payments on the debt they incurred when they fought the Russians on behalf of France. In 1881 CE some Christians from America settled in Palestine and created "America Colony" which was in their minds a Christian utopia in the city of Jerusalem. The same year Baron Edmond Benjamin James de Rothschild decided to do the same thing for Jews and started trying to buy up land so as to create a major Jewish colony in Palestine. However the Ottoman State was wise to this plan and they passed a law forbidding Jews from settling anywhere in Palestine, Jews could live in the

Ottomon empire but Palestine was not a place they could settle, they could visit but they couldn't settle there because zionists were planning a colony and the Ottomons didn't want a Jewish colony in Palestine. Also because Russian Jews were coming in as pilgrims and settling it was feared they were spying for Russia and would act as a future "fifth column". In 1882 CE a few hundred Jews from Yemen arrived in Palestine believing and saying the Jewish Messiah was about to come, he didn't and since they couldn't legally settle they went to go live in caves outside Jerusalem until in 1884 CE a Jewish charity built stone houses for them. From that first year in 1882 CE to 1903 CE about 35,000 Jews from Yemen and East Europe migrated to Palestine and Jewish charities and the wealthy Jewish Rothschild family built places for them to live in. Yet those settlements were illegal and in 1882 CE the Ottomon state even forbid Jews from coming to Palestine. In 1883 CE the Jew Nathan Birnbaum created Kadimah, which was the first Jewish Student Association to promote Zionism. In 1888 CE Europe again pressured the Ottomons to change policies and the Ottomons agreed to allow foreign Jews to settle in Palestine on the condition that they didn't do so en masse. In 1890 CE Nathan Birnbaum was the first one to use the terms "Zionistic", "Zionist" and "Zionism". In 1891 CE the Christian evangelist William Eugene Blackstone went to Palestine and returned to America a firm believer in Zionism. In 1891 CE Blackstone wrote the proto-Zionist Blackstone Memorial of 1891 wherein he urged Americans to help create a Jewish "homeland" in the holy land. This memorial was signed by 413 prominent Christians and a few Jewish leaders in the United States. Blackstone gathered the signatures from people such as John D. Rockefeller, J.P. Morgan, Cyrus McCormick, Senators, Congressmen, religious leaders of all denominations, newspaper editors, the Chief Justice of the U.S. Supreme Court and others. Blackstone then presented the "Memorial" to the American President Harrison in March calling for tacit American support for the creation of a Jewish State in Palestine. Baron Maurice de Hirsch on September 11th, 1891 CE created the Jewish Colonization Association, which was a way for Jews who couldn't afford to move to get the money to move just because they were Jewish. In 1892 CE, the Ottomans decided to prohibit the sale of land in Palestine to Jews, even if they were Ottoman citizens because the situation was getting out of hand with the Jews buying up land and settling there methodically with religious fervor. Thereupon Theodor Herzl concluded Muslims wouldn't sell it, so then how do you get land if the owner of the land doesn't want to sell? In Herzl's diary dated June 1895 CE he wrote, *"We must expropriate gently the private property, [and] spirit the penniless population across the border"* referring to less wealthy non-Jews. In 1895 CE Theodor Herzl wrote an "Address to the Rothschilds" wherein he wanted them to fund a jewish colony in Palestine. Baron Edmond Benjamin James de Rothschild reportedly told him he was unrealistic and his ambitions were too great. On February 14th, 1896 CE Theodor Herzl edited his address to the Rothschilds and published it as a book called "The Jewish State". In March 1897 CE Herzl met the American evangelist William Hechler and told him, " *I must put myself into direct and publicly known relations with a responsible or non responsible ruler– that is, with a minister of state or a prince. Then the Jews will believe in me and follow me. The most suitable personage would be the German Kaiser."* This was quite odd because the German Kaiser Wilhelm II was known as being anti-semitic as early as 1888 CE. Wilhelm II's friend and biographer Lamar Cecil wrote that *"Wilhelm never changed, and throughout his life he believed that Jews were perversely responsible largely through their prominence in the Berlin press and in leftist political movements, for encouraging opposition to his rule."* But alas Germany was in debt as well and debt can make odd things happen. William Hechler then arranged a meeting between Herzl and the uncle of the German Emperor which led to Herzl meeting Kaiser Wilhelm II himself in October, 1898 CE, within the city of Jerusalem itself no less to discuss zionism and whether the German Emperor would help the cause of the Jew Nation through zionism. Later in 1901 CE Theodor Herzl personally met and requested from the Muslim Sultan Abdülhamid II special permission to settle Jews in Palestine, in exchange for 150 million pounds of gold. Now 150 million pounds of gold is a lot of money, look it up yourself and see how much it's worth today, and the Ottomon state was in debt at that time as well, to the Jews Herzl was friends with who promised to forgive the debt if the deal was made. Note it was 150 million <u>pounds</u>, not ounces, an ounce of gold costs $1000+(as I write) and there are 16 ounces in a pound so that's more than a $2.4 trillion offer in gold based on the record low gold prices at the time of this writing. The Muslim Sultan declined the offer refusing to sell even an inch of Palestine saying he has no right to sell it because it doesn't belong to him but belongs to the Ummah(Muslim nation). Shortly after the 1897 CE World Zionist Conference, the Vatican periodical <u>Civilta Cattolica</u> gave its biblical-theological judgement on political Zionism: *"1,827 years have passed since the prediction of Jesus of Nazareth was fulfilled ... that [after the destruction of Jerusalem] the Jews would be led away to be slaves among all the nations and that they would remain in the dispersion [diaspora, galut] until the end of the world. ", " According to the Sacred Scriptures, the Jewish people must always live dispersed and vagabondo [vagrant, wandering] among the other nations, so that they may render witness to Christ not only by the Scriptures ... but by their very existence".* Yet most Catholics today are unaware of this and the Church seems to have changed it's position on Zionism. In 1901 CE the Jewish colonies setup by Edmond James de Rothschild wrote to him saying that his control and sponsorship of them was hindering the colonial endeavor, he got angry and responded *"I created the Jewish Settelements, I alone. Therefore no men, neither colonists nor organizations have the right to interfere in my plans."* In August 1903 CE the British government through L.J. Greenberg offered Theodor Herzl the opportunity to create a autonomous Jewish State governed by Jewish laws in British East Africa and he rejected the offer because it wasn't the holy land. In January 1904 CE Herzl traveled to Rome and spoke with Pope Pius X asking him and the Catholic Church to endorse zionism and the dream of a Jewish state in the holy land. Pope Pius X replied: *"We are unable to favor this movement. We cannot prevent the Jews going to Jerusalem, but we could never sanction it The Jews have not recognized our Lord, therefore we cannot recognize the Jewish people."* Later in 1904 CE Britain, France and Russia entered into an alliance against Germany, while Germany said that French Morocco should become independent of France. In 1906 CE Britain forced the Ottomon State to give the Sinai Peninsula to Egypt, this was due to the business interests both the British and French had invested in the Suez canal project. In 1914 CE the statistics showed the population of Palestine as follows: 657,000 Muslim Arabs(82.6%), 81,000 Christian Arabs (10%), and 59,000 Jews (7.4%). On August 2nd, 1914 CE the German Emperor Wilhem II persuaded the Ottomon State to ally with him and promise to fight against the British and French, however the interesting thing about the German-Ottoman alliance during WWI is that the Ottomon Sultan never signed it because he wanted his nation to remain neutral. Instead it was other high ranking members of the Ottomon military who signed it. Those members of the Ottomon government who did sign to the alliance with Germany were later indicted for treason against the State, but alas it was too late by then and WWI had begun with the Ottomons and Germany and Austria-Hungary against Britain, France, Russia, Serbia, Montenegro, Belgium and Japan. However on September 24th, 1914 CE 5 weeks before Britain declared war on the Ottomons, Lord Kitchener wrote a letter to Abdullah bin Hussein asking how the Sharif family in charge of Mecca and the Arabian Muslim Holy Land would react in case of British war with the Ottomons. The British ambassador in Cairo also wrote to Abdullah bin Hussein saying: "*Since the Ottoman Government disregarded its traditional friendship with Great Britain by joining Britain's enemy, Germany, Britain has no longer the obligation to honor its old traditional ties with Turkey. As such, are you and your majestic father still interested in your initial position to work towards whatever that could lead to the full independence of the Arabs? If yes, then Great Britain is ready to support the Arab movement with every thing that it needs.*" The Sharifi family thereupon clarified that if Britain allied with them then they would fight the Ottomons in the event of war between the two nations. Thereupon on October 31st, 1914 CE the British agreed to the deal and wrote a letter back saying, "*If the Emir of Mecca is willing to assist Great Britain in this conflict, Great Britain is willing, recognizing and respecting the sacred and unique office of Emir Hussein (titles), to guarantee the independence, rights and privileges of the Sharifate against all external foreign aggression, in particular that of the Ottomans.*" ..."*Till now,*"..."*we have defended Islam in the person of the Turks; Henceforward, it shall be in that of the noble Arabs.*" On November 5th, 1914 CE Britain declared war on the Ottomon Empire. Then on November 9th, 1914 CE the British Cabinet discussed the role zionism may play in the war and the Royal Exchequer David Lyold George explicitly referred to the "ultimate destiny of Palestine" as fitting into a zionist framework. Germany stationed troops in Palestine and the reactions amongst the Jews living there to WWI was commented upon by the German general Friedrich Freiherr Kress von Kressenstein, *"How curious that the war has brought about an upsurge in the struggle between the Zionists and the non-Zionists, a battle that has turned ugly and done little to further the interests of Jews in general. The non-Zionists, that is to say those Jews who had no political objectives and who belonged to the Orthodox current, at the time the preponderant majority in Palestine. The Zionists residing there represented no more than 5 percent of the population, but were very active and fanatical, and terrorized the non-Zionists. During the war, the non-Zionists attempted to free themselves from the Zionist terror with the aid of the Turks. They rightly feared that the activities of the Zionists would destroy their good relations that prevailed amongst long-time Jewish residents in Palestine and the Arabs."* On November 11th, 1914 CE the Ottomons declared a "Jihad" against the WWI allied powers and urged the Sharifi family to join the fight against Britain. In January 1915 CE the zionist Herbert Samuel presented a memorandum to the British government on how Britain would benefit if it took over Palestine and allowed Jewish immigration to that place. Throughout the rest of 1915 CE Britain and the Sharif family plotted on how they would divide the middle east after the war. However in December 1915 CE the British made a deal with Ibn Saud who ruled the middle and eastern desert area of Arabia, and had been at war with the Ottomons since 1904 CE, giving him a similar deal as they gave to the Sharifi family with neither family knowing about the deals the other made with Britain. In February 1916 CE Colonel Mark Sykes wrote Herbert Samuel suggesting it might be better if Belgium ruled Palestine so that Britain could avoid tension with France over the issue since France wanted to rule Palestine themselves and in response Samuel replied: *"By excluding Hebron and the East of the Jordan there is less to discuss with the Moslems, as the*

Mosque of Omar then becomes the only matter of vital importance to discuss with them and further does away with any contact with the bedouins, who never cross the river except on business. I imagine that the principal object of Zionism is the realization of the ideal of an existing center of nationality rather than boundaries or extent of territory." Afterwards in May 1916 CE Britain and France secretly agreed to the Sykes-Picot agreement to divide the middle east which unbeknownst to the Sharifi and Ibn Saud families contradicted the deals they thought they had with Britain. So under the impression Britain's deal with them was real, the Sharifi family revolted against the Ottomons in June 1916 CE and the Arabian Peninsula fought the Ottomons under the influence of the British T.E. Laurence who had previously attended "Jesus College" at Oxford from 1907-1910 CE. I'm not joking T.E. Lawrence actually went to "Jesus College", it's a real college. In 1917 CE the Saud family and the Sharifi family fought each other over Arabia, with each side thinking Britain was on their side and wanted them to rule. In the midst of all this the British foreign secretary Arthur Balfour stated in the Balfour Declaration on November 2nd, 1917 CE: "*The four great powers are committed to Zionism, and Zionism, be it right or wrong, good or bad, is rooted in age-long tradition, in present needs, in future hopes, of far profounder import than the desires and prejudices of the...Arabs who now inhabit that ancient land.*" Weeks later on December 9, 1917 CE British soldiers entered Jerusalem after defeating the Muslim Ottomon army who abandoned the city, coincidentally the first day of Hannukah started that very night at sunset. While later dismissed as a false rumor when Muslims throughout the British empire began to rebel and demand independence, it was initially widely reported across the world that the British general who conquered Jerusalem, Edmund Allenby, had entered Jerusalem with a bible in one hand and a crucifix in the other loudly and joyously proclaiming

17

"*Today the wars of the crusaders are completed.*" Then just as suddenly as it started, on November 4th 1918 CE Austria-Hungary agreed to peace. Meanwhile the German army staged a coup to overthrow Wilhelm II and faced with sudden mutiny he was forced to abdicate his rule on November 9th 1918 CE. Immediately afterwards on November 11th, 1918 CE which was exactly 4 solar years after the Ottomons declared a Jihad against the allied powers, the treaty of Versailles ended WWI. Germans were furious and felt betrayed by their revolting military because they were winning in Europe especially after the Russians left the war, that was until the Americans entered the picture and the allies began to win in Europe in July 1918 CE. But still Germans thought they would win and many were outraged such a peace was agreed to, especially when it was by a government that had just mutinied it's way into power 2 days before. It was certainly a crazy end to a crazy war which had initially begun under crazy circumstances as well. Yet one fascinating aspect is that the US president Woodrow Wilson had made it known that no peace treaty could be signed if Wilhelm II was in charge of Germany. Why did Wilson not want Wilhelm II to be present at any peace table? That is not known. Later on in 1919 CE Wilhelm II denounced his abdication to the star top German general born of common stock who remained loyal, Marshal August von Mackenson, saying it was the "*deepest, most disgusting shame ever perpetrated by a person in history, the Germans have done to themselves... egged on and misled by the tribe of Judah...Let no German ever forget this, nor rest until these parasites have been destroyed and exterminated from German soil!*" Wilhelm II further proposed Jews were a "*nuisance that humanity must get rid of some way or other. I believe the best thing would be gas!*" Yet later despite making such remarks, when Adolf Hitler later rose to prominence and seemed to be following such a philosophy Wilhem II remarked *"I am ashamed to be a German."* and August von Mackenson was also unsupportive of the Nazi Regime and accused of treason. So that's one historical anomaly in that Wilhelm II meets the Jewish Zionist Theodor Herzl in 1898 CE who wants Germany to help him create a Jewish State in Palestine. Then Wilhelm II leads Germany into WWI 16 years later getting the Ottomons to join him, even though the Sultan never agreed to the alliance but his military did. Then Wilhelm II's military revolts less than a year after the Ottomons lose Palestine and he abdicates only to denounce his abdication the next year blaming the Jews for all of Germany's woes. Then when Hitler follows his suggested solution to Jews he disavows him and feels ashamed of his national legacy before dying in 1941 CE well before WWII was over and it seemed as though Nazis would win. I'm not saying there was a conspiracy but it'd be very interesting to know what the zionist Herzl and Wilhelm II discussed in 1898 CE, when they met in Jerusalem. Whether Wilhelm II intended to help zionism or not, his actions and even his suggestions facilitated the goals that Theodor Herzl had despite being known as staunchly anti-semitic. It's very ironic. In the beginning, middle and end Wilhelm II hated Jews but in the middle he hated Germany and he also hated being German in the end despite his own suggestions for Germany's future treatment of Jews being implemented by Adolf Hitler. Since he blamed the Jews for Germany's woes and hated himself and his actions and plans for Germany then it seems possible Herzl might have had some leverage over Wilhelm II other than financial that could've made Wilhelm II help zionism despite hating Jews. What could that be? Well the rumor is Wilhelm II was a sodomite, but I must repeat that is an unsubstantiated rumor that can never be definitively proven despite what evidence suggests. However if true then a masterful conspiracy could be possible. The best clue perhaps is that Theodor Herzl said in 1897 CE that Wilhelm II would be the best candidate to further Zionist goals. Whereas on paper it makes little sense for Herzl to say that especially about an anti-semite, unless of course Herzl used blackmail of the type that could destroy a Emperor's life in total. Just imagine, what would you do if you were the emperor of Germany in 1897 CE and a Jew threatened to reveal you were a sodomite unless you took actions that helped create a Jewish state in Palestine? Would such a threat be enough to push someone to trigger WWI through their actions and WWII through their suggestions and thus ruin their historical legacy and nation? It's possible. Such a scenario where Wilhelm II hated Jews, blamed Jews for controlling the government and ruining Germany and hated being German but loved Germany would then make sense. Otherwise Wilhelm II is just one crazy character from history who has contradictory beliefs. Don't get paranoid, that's just some speculative theory that makes history lessons more fun to learn, but valid or not such a theory does teach us how powerful vices can potentially be and why we shouldn't have sinful habits ourselves. Afterall you never want to be in a position where your sins can be used against you to cause you to do more sins thinking it will somehow be worth it. Just think though how, if Wilhelm II was a secret sodomite then his sodomous indulgences may have been the causes of both WWI, WWII and many other things that continue to effect us today. That's sodomy, you never know how dangerous it can be. At the least we can say Herzl had to have made a powerful offer to Wilhelm II in order for him to help the Zionist cause. Remember Herzl was a man who offered to eliminate Ottomon debt and pay the Sultan 150 million pounds of gold for the sake of a Jewish state, and that was 6 years after Herzl had already concluded Muslims wouldn't sell Palestine. So if that's the type of offer Herzl makes to those he thinks will not cooperate then what kind of offer do you think Herzl made to Wilhelm II when he thought he was the most likely and most able to help the cause of Zionism? Note the offer need not have been legitimate, all it need be is enough to get Wilhelm II to comply with Herzl's zionist desires whether Herzl actually followed through or could follow through on what he promised Wilhelm II in exchange for compliance is irrelevant. Regardless of whether Wilhelm II and Theodor Herzl were co-conspirators it seems obvious that Britain, France and/or Russia were in some type of cahoots to a certain extent against the Ottomons in favor of zionism. Germany need not have been in on it I just speculate on the possibility, however don't let that speculation discount the clear evidence of British and French zionist scheming. A conspiracy is simply a secret plan which secretive parties have to do something. One can conspire for good or evil purposes, a conspiracy is simply a secret plan. Technically zionism cannot be called a conspiracy because it was never a secret. Since the Crusades it was known that the Christian world didn't want Muslims in charge of Palestine. Zionism is basically just an alternative form of Crusading except its purportedly done by Jews and they don't care about getting religious conversions. People just didn't pay attention to it and it achieved a lot that it set out to achieve before many knew of it. Even today few are aware of the word zionism let alone it's meaning or history. On December 5, 1918 CE (St. Nicholas day) the "Eastern Committee of the Cabinet" met to discuss Palestine and what would happen to it. Notable Brits were present including, Lord Curzon, General Jan Smuts, Lord Balfour, Lord Robert Cecil, General Sir Henry Wilson, Chief of the Imperial General Staff, representatives of the Foreign Office, the India Office, the Admiralty, the War

Office, and the Treasury; as well as T. E. Lawrence. The minutes tell that Lord Curzon stated: "*The Palestine position is this. If we deal with our commitments, there is first the general pledge to Hussein in October 1915, under which Palestine was included in the areas as to which Great Britain pledged itself that they should be Arab and independent in the future . . . the United Kingdom and France – Italy subsequently agreeing – committed themselves to an international administration of Palestine in consultation with Russia, who was an ally at that time . . .A new feature was brought into the case in November 1917, when Mr. Balfour, with the authority of the War Cabinet, issued his famous declaration to the Zionists that Palestine 'should be the national home of the Jewish people, but that nothing should be done – and this, of course, was a most important proviso – to prejudice the civil and religious rights of the existing non-Jewish communities in Palestine. Those, as far as I know, are the only actual engagements into which we entered with regard to Palestine.*" Meaning Britain admittedly made 3 different contradictory deals regarding Palestine before they had it and then they got it and everybody expected them to keep the deal they made, all the deals they made with everyone simply couldn't be kept. They even ignored deals they made with others as well intentionally using spokesmen who knew of deals without knowing the details to say "*those are the only deals we made, as far as I know.*" Since they couldn't make all 3 deals and knew this when they made them then we must wonder why they made deals they knew they wouldn't and couldn't keep and what was the deal they planned to keep? To answer that lets just look at the least needed deal and the most recent and we would identify the deal with the zionists to be the least necessary to be made and the most recent. Thereby if there were a conspiracy, and a government making multiple deals about what to do with a territory before they conquer it is the stuff of conspiracy, then it would seem that the zionist plan was conspiratorial.

But wait have you forgotten that in 1841 CE Charles Churchill as the British ambassador to the Ottomon empire encouraged the Jews to seek Palestine and promised Britain would aid the Zionists toward that end? Well that happened. So when Britain made that deal with Zionists in 1841 CE and then "coincidentally" end up in control of Palestine 77 years later with 3 plans, one of which matches the 1841 plan, it is pretty natural to suspect that maybe Britain had always been planning to conquer Palestine for the Jews like they said in 1841 CE. But why then hide this plan? Why not take pride in the success? That's where the conspiratorial theme comes in, due to conspiracies being secretive because the secrecy is believed to be crucial to success. But I leave that to you to decide. Would the Zionist plan be aided by governmental secrecy or not? Remember the plan involves one of the world's smallest and most hated minorities, Jews, becoming owners of the most religiously valued land in the world that has seen centuries of warfare fought for it's soil by members of rival faiths other than Judaism. So would secrecy benefit such a plan? If not secrecy then what about denial? Of course the Arabs had these suspicions of conspiracy for zionism and so they accused those parties they deemed guilty. In response to inquiries about their plans for Palestine the World Zionist Organization issued a statement: *"We ask that Palestine be constituted as a free and independent state, to be governed under a democratic form of government recognizing no distinction of creed or race or ethnic descent, and with adequate power to protect the country against oppression of any kind. We do not wish to see Palestine, either now or at any time in the future, organized as a Jewish state."* With statements like that you would not think they were at that very moment drawing maps of a future Jewish State in the region of Palestine. Or would you? I mean today there is a Jewish State in Palestine, named Israel, I guess Zionists didn't mean it when they said *"at any time in the future"*.

During the spring of 1919 CE the "League of Nations" was designed to deal with issues just like the one the world faced with Palestine. They setup a commission to decide who would get what out of the ruins of the Ottomon Empire. This commission reported back to US President Woodrow Wilson on the matter of Zionism and said, "*Not only you as president but the American people as a whole should realize that if the American government decided to support the establishment of a Jewish state in Palestine, they are committing the American people to the use of force in that area, since only by force can a Jewish state in Palestine be established or maintained.*" After WWI the Zionists and Christians made plans to divy up the Holy Land and a map circulated, it was made by a Reverand Clarence Larkin showing the borders of the Zionist state allegedly decreed by the bible. Fortunately I recently obtained a copy of this map while reading a book published in 2007 CE by a certain Christian Pastor of a megachurch in Texas which has 20,000 active members who also runs a evangelist tv network with his own tv shows seen by 150 million worldwide. The first edition of this book of his was published in 2005 CE and sold 700,000 copies. It basically said that Islam = Terrorism and all Christians and Americans should support God's Chosen people of Israel and kill all those Jihadi Muslims who believe in the Quran. He said those Muslims who don't believe in the Quran can be allowed to live. He used the bible to justify his positions while simultaneously saying Christianity is better than Islam because it is so peaceful and tolerant. He wrote that Christians and Jews must cooperate to kill all the Muslims in order to preserve the peaceful biblical/American way of life. This Christian has personally met and advised every Prime Minister of Israel since 1977 CE. Anyways he used this map, first made on January 18th, 1919 CE, to show the minimum amount of land which he says the biblical

Christian God decreed is Israel according to the biblical book of Genesis; or so he says:

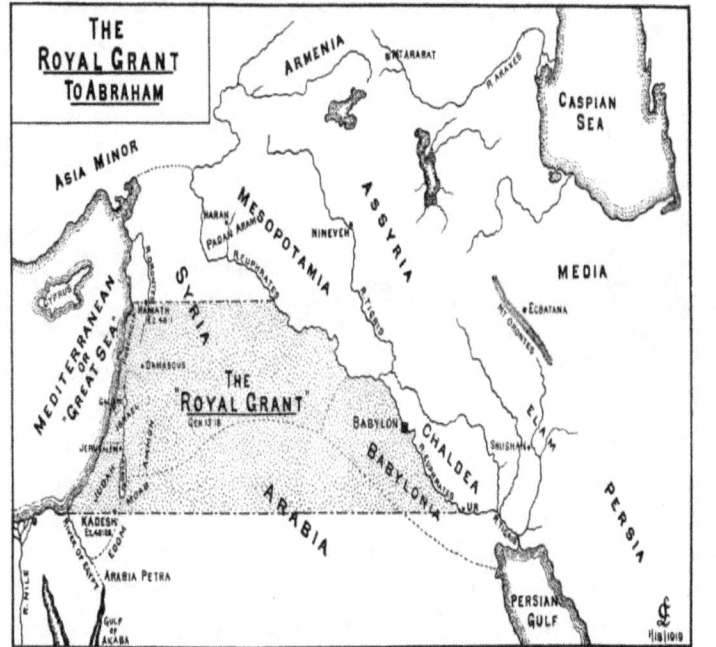

Currently this proposed map of Israel includes territiory that is now part of Palestine, Jordan, Lebanon, Syria, Iraq, and Saudi Arabia. As you can imagine those Muslimish countries today don't really want to give their countries away. Ironically most Muslims don't even know about such a map/blueprint. Remember that map was made in 1919 CE, over 20 years before WWII and is still being cited as a legal divine endowment by Christians supporting Israel who advise it's Prime Ministers. But that map isn't the Jewish map, it's the Christian map of what Christians say Israel is supposed to be, the Jewish map of what the "Promised Land" is, is different. One map in Hebrew shows a little more territory in the Jewish vision of Israel which they believe God has decreed to be their country.

25

גבולות 'מסעי' – גבולות התנחלות השבטים

But alas this Hebrew map is just one version that while expanding upon the Christian version, since it adds the Sinai Peninsula, more of Lebanon, more of Syria and more of Iraq, this is still just one version of Israel. Sadly that version is the small version. Zionists have even bigger plans and consider such a large amount of territory becoming Israel to be too little. As Theodor Herzl wrote in his diary way back in 1904 CE Volume 2 page 711 when he stated that the future Jewish Israeli state is from "*The Brook of Egypt to the Euphrates*". Some conspiratorial personalities have alleged this is precisely what the 2 blue lines on the Israeli flag represent, one blue line representing the Nile River the other representing the Euphrates River with Israel in between. But that claim cannot be proven, and when people cite it the Israeli desire for the land between the Nile and the Euphrates is often dismissed as conspiracy simply because of the flag symbolism being unverifiable. Yet regardless of what the two blue lines on the Israeli flag symbolize it's a solid fact that Israelis religiously believe God wants them to rule the land between the Nile and the Euphrates rivers. So the flag is irrelevant to the issue, but unfortunately many who try to cite the Israeli flag to prove the issue end up making the issue seem fictional when the geographical desires are documented facts. However Herzl's writings were not translated into english until 1952 CE, so unless you knew Hebrew or German you had no way to know what the Zionist Jew Theodor Herzl was actually preaching to Jews about establishing a Jewish state in the Holy Land. Which makes it interesting considering how Germans treated Jews from 1904-1952 CE when they were practically the only non-Hebrew speaking people who could read and understand Herzl's writings. But does that mean the world had an excuse to be clueless? No. This is because in his testimony to a special U.N. commission on July 9th, 1947 CE Rabbi Fischmann publicly clarified Jewish/ Zionist beliefs and plans when he said: "***The Promised Land extends from the River of Egypt up to the Euphrates, it includes parts of Syria and Lebanon.***" So while the Christian map for Israel in 1919 is quite larger than the modern day map, the Jewish map of 1904 and 1947 CE is even larger than the Christian version. The 1947 CE Jewish/Zionist map for Israel is even larger than the other one and includes Kuwait and part of Turkey:

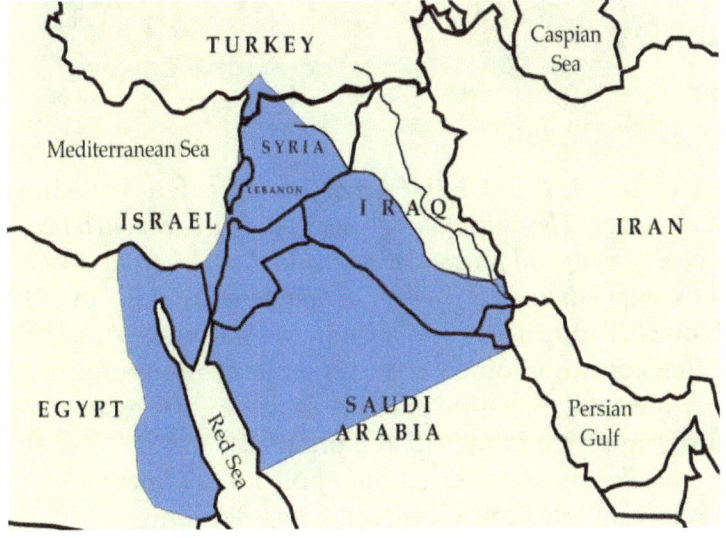

So this is just something to keep in mind when you hear on the news that Israel wants peace and has no plans for expansion.   Yet not to be outdone by this map, the Christians also have a big version of "Greater Israel" which they extrapolate from the books of Psalms, Daniel, Ezekial, Numbers and the New Testament book titled as "Revelation".   The big Christian map of Israel is shown below and includes Cyprus and more parts of Turkey:

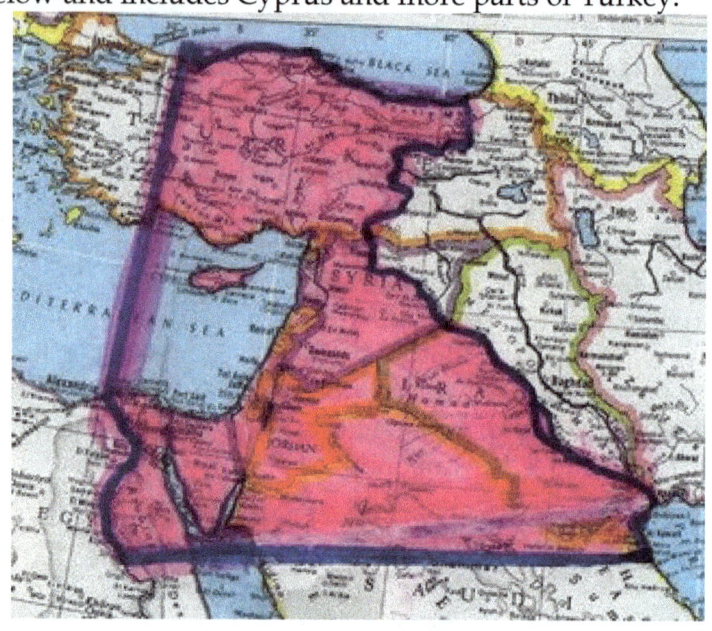

On March 3rd, 1919 CE the American President Woodrow Wilson said: "*The allied nations with the fullest concurrence of our government and people are agreed that in Palestine shall be laid the foundations of a Jewish Commonwealth.*" Also in 1919 CE Jewish Scouting for kids began in Palestine, while Jews in other countries joined Scouting organizations and made many Jew-only Scouting groups. In 1922 CE the League of Nations approved the British Balfour declaration to be the template for future international policies on Palestine. Then Jewish boy scouts joined the Israeli Zionist paramilitary organization Haganah which had been made in 1921 CE to be a type of Jewish security service for Jews in Palestine. In 1922 CE the U.S. Congress extended sympathies to Jews worldwide and unanimously passed an endorsement of the Balfour Declaration with the House of Foreign Affairs stating, "*The Jews of America are profoundly interested in establishing a National Home in the ancient land for their race. Indeed, this is the ideal of the Jewish people, everywhere, for, despite their dispersion, Palestine has been the object of their veneration since they were expelled by the Romans. For generations they have prayed for the return to Zion. During the past century this prayer has assumed practical form.*" Meanwhile the legislatures in 33 states, representing 85% of the population, adopted resolutions favoring the creation of a Jewish state in Palestine. Governors of 37 states, 54 United States senators, and 250 congressmen signed petitions to the President advocating this cause. They did this in 1922 CE. Prior to that from 1917 CE -1922 CE Britain and France diplomatically split the middle east making Palestine an internationally governed state via a British mandate. During which time it looked like:

In 1922 CE Britain gave the World Zionist organization the mandate to administer Jewish immigration and settlement in Palestine; this immigration and settlement was funded primarily by American Jews and Zionists. Problems occurred due to this so in 1923 CE Palestine was divided into Palestine and Transjordan.

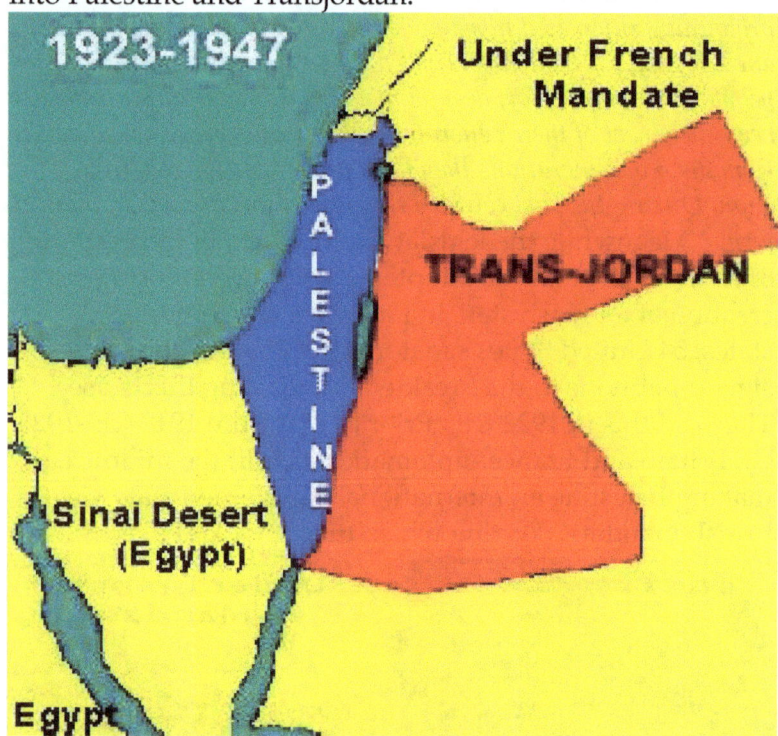

In 1931 CE a Jewish guerrilla group Irgun was made, which had broken off from Haganah because they thought Haganah wasn't violent enough and showed too much restraint when "protecting Jews" from Arab security threats. However a Jewish State could not be created in a land with a Jewish minority, so in 1937 CE David Ben-Gurion (who later became the first prime minister of Israel) wrote to his son: *The Arabs will have to go*". Coincidentally in the very same year, Lord Peel of the Palestinian Royal

Commission proposed a "2-state solution" in the Holy Land where Palestine would be split into a Jew State, Arab State and a British zone. This plan to divide Palestine was proposed in 1937 CE, years before WWII took place.

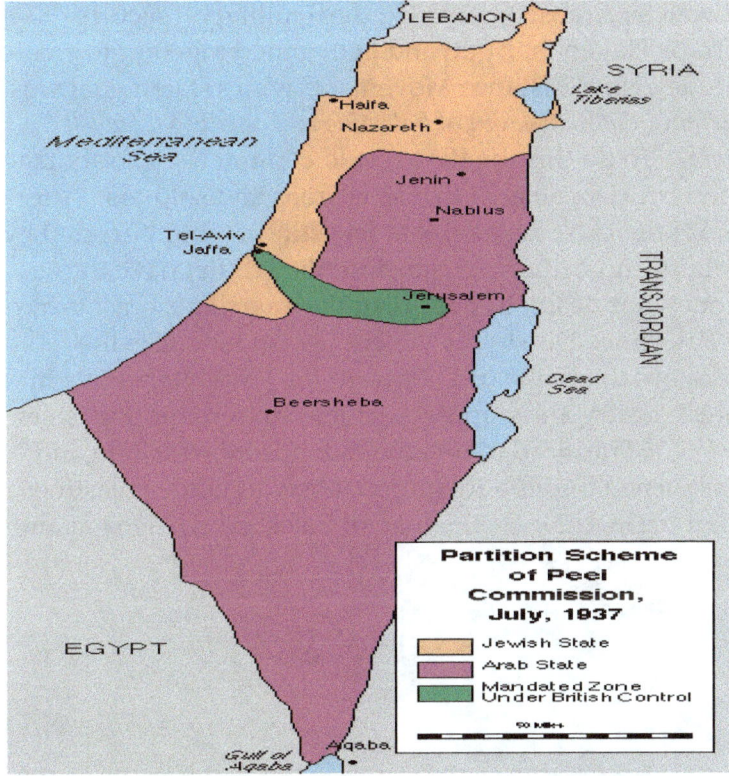

In 1940 CE a group of Jews split off from the extremist Irgun group and formed a group called Lehi which waged war against Britain. Lehi did this because in 1939 CE Britain had restricted Jewish emigration to Palestine since the Jews were causing problems in Palestine that led to violent altercations and pressure from Palestinians to stop letting violent Jews into their country which Britain had done since 1922 CE due to Americans funding. Irgun agreed with Lehi in fighting the British for restricting

Jewish emigration but didn't want to do so while Britain was fighting Germany in WWII. In 1944 CE the Irgun group declared war against British Palestine and they launched a campaign of terrorism targeting British citizens as well as Arabs. In 1945 CE the 3 military/"security" groups Haganah, Irgun and Lehi joined together to create the "Jewish Resistance Movement" who's stated goal was *"driving the British out of Palestine and creating a Jewish State"*. To do this the JRM would commit acts of sabotage and terrorism against British citizens and soldiers. After WWII the U.N. decided that Palestine should be ceded by Britain, and Britain agreed since they didn't have the money nor desire to put down the guerrilla zionist groups in Palestine. Due to the violent Jewish terrorists the transjordan people did not want the Jewish terrorists in their country and opposed the Jewish immigration, so in 1946 CE Transjordan became indepedent of Britain and was turned into the Kingdom of Jordan while Palestine went to the U.N. So the map of Palestine changed again:

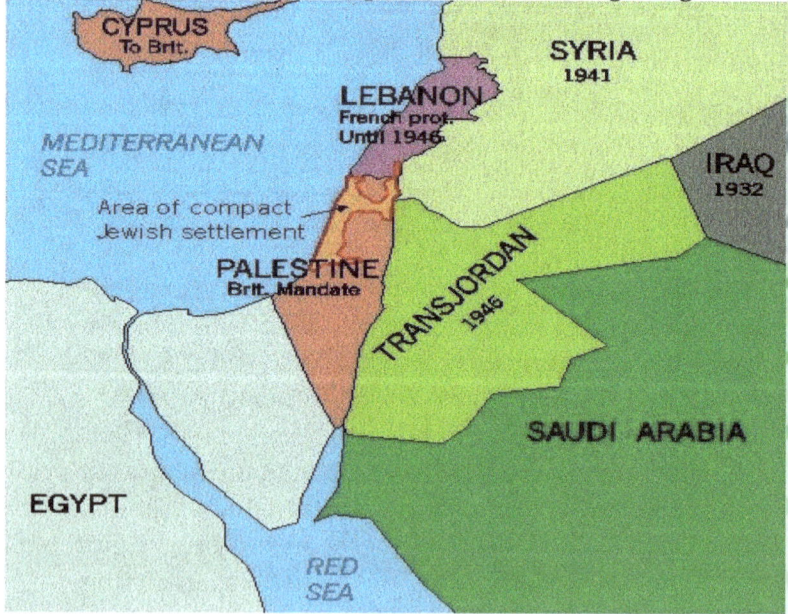

32

In 1947 CE the U.N. declared that an exclusively Jewish State should be created in the holy land. A Partition Plan in late 1947 CE was announced marking which land would go to Jews and which land would go to Palestinians once Britian withdrew it's forces the next year. The 2 U.N. Partion plans were as follows:

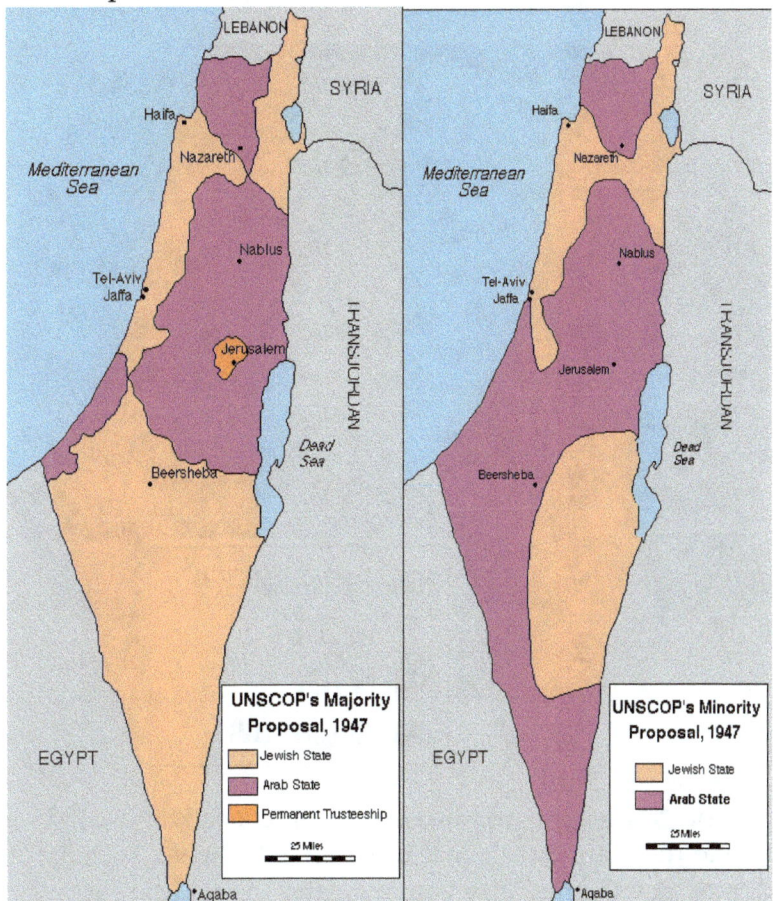

The UN voted on the majority plan (above left) before it became official. The minority plan(above right) was not voted on but was the backup plan if the majority plan didn't pass the UN democratic decision making process. Coincidentally both plans amounted to a fulfillment of

Charles Churchill's 1841 CE plan to make Palestine a Jewish State proposed 106 solar years earlier. Why do you think Winston Churchill didn't say his grandfather's plan came true? Winston knew history but he also knew others don't. However its unknown history that's most important.

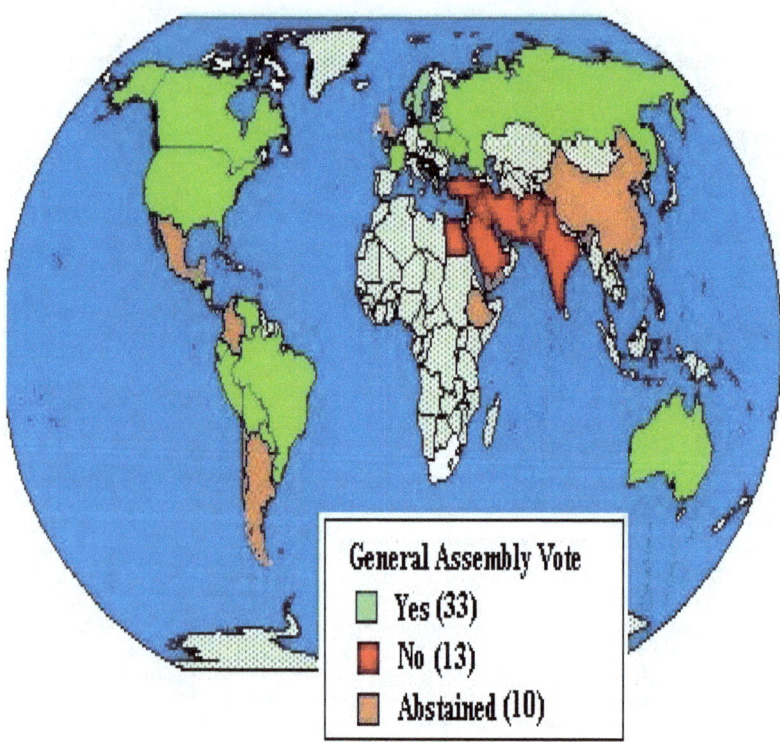

As you can see the middle east region collectively voted NO to the plan, but since it was 33 Yes to 13 No, because of democracy the majority vote won and the middle east was told YES is the answer to the establishment of a Jewish state in the middle east. Now compare the map showing actual Jewish land ownership in Palestine(orange) in 1947 CE with the UN plan to create the Jewish state of Israel in 1948 CE and tell me if it seems equitable.

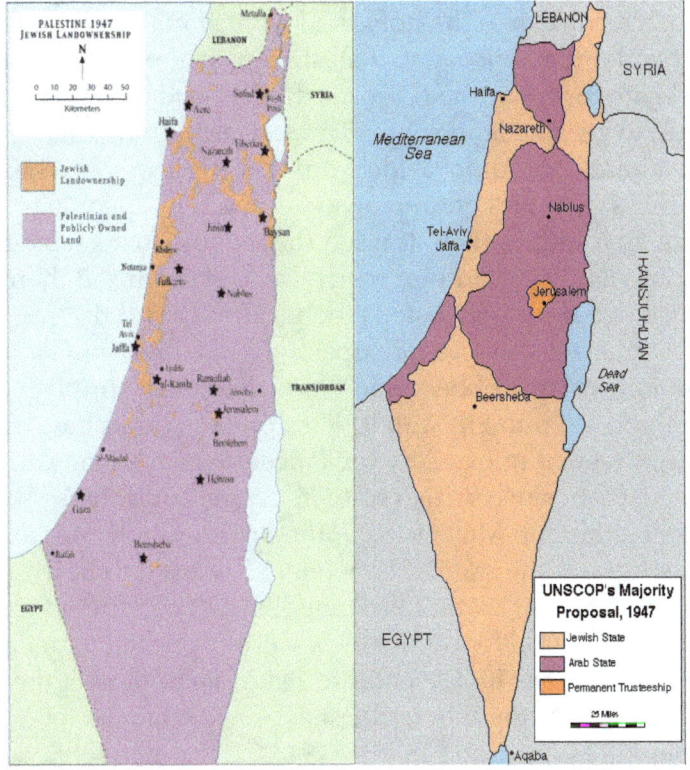

As you can clearly see the UN Majority Plan essentially gave lots of holy land to Jews which was already owned and occupied by non-Jews. However that's just what the U.N. said was going to happen if everything went according to their plans. Before the UN partition took place the Jewish groups Haganah, Irgun and Lehi reorganized into a professional regular army known as the IDF (Israeli Defense Force) and started fighting the Palestinian people for land. First Haganah split up into Haganah and Irgun and then Irgun split into Irgun and Lehi, but then Haganah+Irgun+Lehi rejoined as the group called JRM and in 1947-48 JRM became the IDF. The IDF would kill non-Jewish people if they didn't move and give up their land. Technically speaking this was widescale

Jewish terrorism in the holy land against non-Jews just years after the Holocaust. Palestinians complained about the brute force but the IDF said the UN said they were going to get that land soon so there was nothing the Palestinians could do, aside from leave. However when the IDF saw it was getting away with forcing people to leave their homes they decided they would just keep on stealing land beyond that which the UN promised them. Which of course was 2 steps too far legally and the Palestinians got even more upset. The UN was not oblivious to this robbery and bloodshed, they simply didn't do anything to stop it. To stop the crimes the Arab nations were requested by the Palestinians to come and protect them since British soldiers weren't and the U.N. wasn't either. In May 1948 CE the British withdrew from Palestine and the state of Israel declared itself to be a official state, but by that time the IDF had conquered more land than the U.N. said the Jews were supposed to get and the Arab nations had went into Palestine to protect the non-Jews from the IDF terrorists. Hence when Israel declared it's statehood in May 1948 CE the map looked like this:

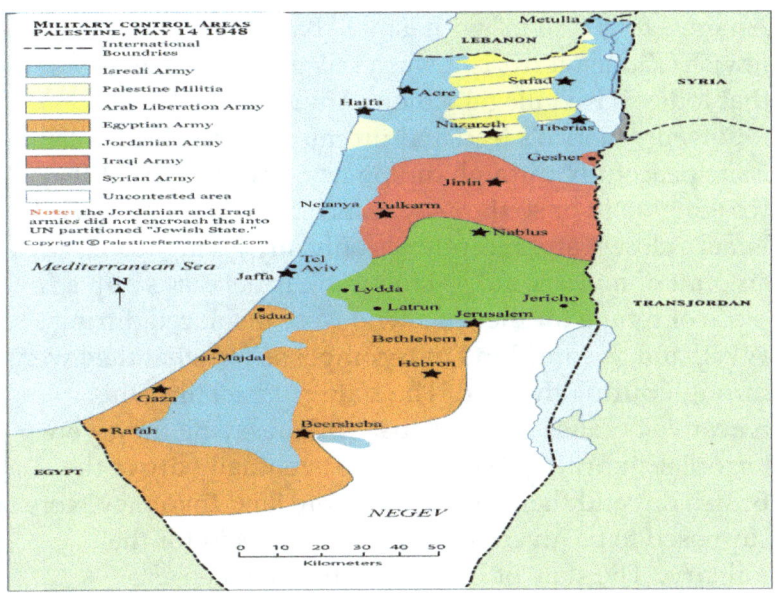

Now the U.N. didn't know what to do, because the state of Israel the U.N. said would be allowed to exist was claiming control over land which the U.N. said was Palestine, meanwhile the Egyptian and Jordanian army was occupying some of what the U.N. said was Israel because the non-Jewish people there were getting killed by the terrorist organization known as IDF which had just declared itself to be the military of Israel. The IDF was formed by 3 terrorist groups and then it officially became the military of the state of Israel, legally recognized throughout the world overnight. Thus the IDF provided the blueprints for terrorists dreaming of statehood. Currently the IDF is still the military of Israel. America was the first entity in the entire world to recognize the state of Israel and say it was legitimate, President Truman recognized Israel and declared it to be America's ally 11 minutes after the Israeli state itself declared it's statehood on May 14th, 1948 CE. All it took was 11 minutes for

America to go "all in" with Israel. Back then Jewish/Zionist terrorism wasn't illegal and some may say that today it isn't illegal either. Anyways the U.N. followed America's lead and promised to resolve the land issue peacefully through diplomacy, and they are still working on it; or so they say. Since then America has been Israel's closest and recently it's only ally giving it a large amount of military aid. Many think Israel was setup as a place of refuge for the Jews who were displaced during WWII and as some kind of recompense for what they went through during the war. The state of Israel likes this narrative because it's much better than saying they were terrorists in British Palestine who eventually drove the British out and then conquered more land than they were supposed to be given because America paid for their military. The state of Israel prefers to be seen as a international victim made by holocaust survivors, instead of being known as terrorists who got away with stealing a state. Personally I think the number of 6 million Jews alleged to have been killed during WWII is grossly exaggerated anyways, because the World Almanac of 1940 CE says there were 15,319,359 Jews in the world at that time and in 1948 CE it says there were 15,763,630 Jews in the world. This means there were more Jews after WWII than existed before, how could that be possible if 40% of them were allegedly killed during those 8 years? It is rather difficult to tell what religious background a skeleton has, especially during the 1940s CE before DNA analysis was used, so it seems to have been an effective public relations campaign spun by the Jewish owners of media outlets capitalizing on the opportunity to create a Jewish State, which Jews were actively fighting for in Palestine during WWII. I'm not a "Holocaust Denier", I do believe civilians were systematically killed by Nazis, Soviets and the Allied Powers during WWII. The thing that I dispute is the number of Jews who were killed. Studies have shown the number 6 million is far too high and such things do matter a lot, especially if such numbers are going to be influencing modern beliefs and actions such as how to deal with the Palestine issue. The thing isn't whether Jews died or not, the thing is why have lies been told about more Jews being killed than actually were and how has the lie about the number of Jews who died effected the world? Numbers do matter, of course 1 is too many but to say the number doesn't matter as long as it happened is to cheapen the truth and accept falsehood. I mean if the number of Jews who died really doesn't matter why stop at 6 million, lets say Hitler killed 999 trillion. Why don't we? Because we know that's not true and we know what kind of influence such a fiction would have on how Jews are treated if the inflated number were used. Basically my issue with the Holocaust crowd is that today they treat Jews as though they are an endangered species or something while in the Holy Land they are mercilessly butchering members of the human species. It's like a farmer praising ancient wolves for having survived a bear attack that happened last century while the descendants of those wolves who survived are currently eating his livestock and poultry. The WWII Holocaust is over, the one in Palestine is ongoing and Zionists/Jews are the perpetrators. Yes Jews were victims in the past, but today they are the criminals and they are getting away with more heinous crimes than Hitler did to Jews because people keep treating Jews as though they are victims because of Hitler. Justice means they don't get special treatment due to past events. To dwell on the Holocaust is to make it even more damaging. Even if millions of Jews were systematically slaughtered in Europe during WWII what does that have to do with the Palestinian people? Why should Palestinians be punished because of it? At that time the Jews were less than a third of the Palestinian population and during WWII they were killing British and Palestinian soldiers and civilians with impunity. But then WWII ended and suddenly these Jewish terrorists in Palestine were declared to be the owners of private property that had been in Christian and Muslim families for centuries, because some other Jews in Europe got killed. The Christians and Muslims were instantly made homeless and some were physically removed from their homes forced to leave their possessions behind never to return. They became refugees and their land has been occupied to this day with new generations being born since then further complicating the problem, since now there are people who claim birthright over stolen property; similar to how the situation was in South Africa. What is even worse than the media misrepresentation and false history being indoctrinated in American schools, is that many Christian organizations are fundraising for Israel and think that it's a Jew vs. Muslim situation not realizing that they are supporting a country that is slaughtering Christian men, women and children. How can one consider themselves to be Christian and give money to Jews in Palestine (the land where Jesus pbuh taught) to kill Christians? The very existence of Israel as a state would be comparable to the U.N. forcing the United States to cede the entire state of oil-richTexas to Australian aborigines because of their systematic elimination by the British colonists, completely ignoring the Mexican claims to Texas and the Americans and Mexicans currently living there. Surely Mexicans and Americans can see how unjust that would be yet this is what has been done in Palestine; which is also one of the world's most religiously significant regions. This is where the difference between peace and justice becomes apparent. Whereas since the Israeli IDF took more land than the UN planned to partition to them and were killing non-Jewish people because they weren't Jewish the Arab armies invaded to protect the Palestinian people and decrease the size of the Israeli state run by Zionist terrorists. But Israel having America as it's ally officially since May was able to counterattack in July 1948 and ended up not only getting back their stolen land but even more. This is what happened to the map of Palestine from 1947-1948 CE, showing the UN proposed plan in 1947, what the map was in June 1948 after Israel was "invaded" and what happened in July 1948 after Israel expanded through warfare paid for mainly by US donations + taxdollars.

| 1947: United Nations Partition Plan | June 1948: Arab armies invade | July 1948: Israeli army counterattacks |

Later in 1956 CE war broke out again, this time between Britain, France and Israel vs. Egypt. This was because Egypt blockaded Israel's port Eliat thereby cutting off Israeli trade through the gulf of Aqaba and Red Sea, and nationalized the Suez Canal taking it away from Britain/France. The Egyptian military lost and Israeli forces occupied the Sinai Peninsula.

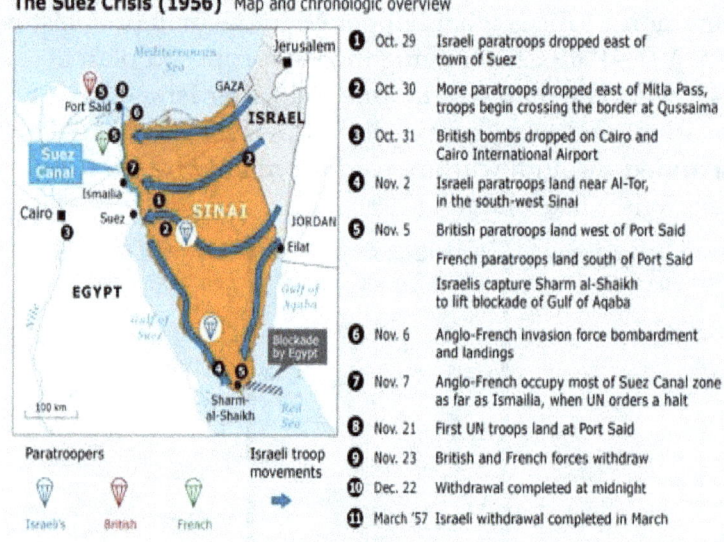

The Suez Crisis (1956) Map and chronologic overview

❶	Oct. 29	Israeli paratroops dropped east of town of Suez
❷	Oct. 30	More paratroops dropped east of Mitla Pass, troops begin crossing the border at Qussaima
❸	Oct. 31	British bombs dropped on Cairo and Cairo International Airport
❹	Nov. 2	Israeli paratroops land near Al-Tor, in the south-west Sinai
❺	Nov. 5	British paratroops land west of Port Said
		French paratroops land south of Port Said
		Israelis capture Sharm al-Shaikh to lift blockade of Gulf of Aqaba
❻	Nov. 6	Anglo-French invasion force bombardment and landings
❼	Nov. 7	Anglo-French occupy most of Suez Canal zone as far as Ismailia, when UN orders a halt
❽	Nov. 21	First UN troops land at Port Said
❾	Nov. 23	British and French forces withdraw
❿	Dec. 22	Withdrawal completed at midnight
⓫	March '57	Israeli withdrawal completed in March

After the 1956 occupation of Sinai, Israel returned the peninsula to Egypt after policies were changed. 11 years later Egypt and Israel were at war again but this time Israel started it. You see the Palestinians didn't really have their own national infrastructure, the Palestinian territory bordering Jordan was claimed as Jordan territory and the Gaza Strip bordering Egypt was claimed as Egyptian territory. Since both Egypt and Jordan had gotten that out of the 1948 war they considered it legally their territory, not Palestine. Whereas Israel decided to take that territory for themselves so they attacked the Egyptian Gaza Strip and told the country of Jordan to "mind it's own business". But Jordan did not do that. Instead Jordan and Syria attacked Israel because Israel attacked Egypt. However

Israel having the latest equipment from America and Egypt, Jordan and Syria having out of date technology, they famously lost the war of 1967 CE in just 6 days. Which to Jews seemed like a miracle but logistically was easily predictable because at that time the Arab nations simply thought Arabism and numbers would win wars when in reality numbers and national/racial pride means nothing.

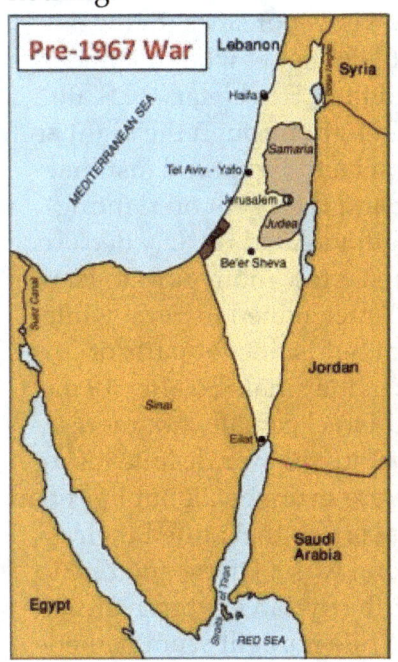
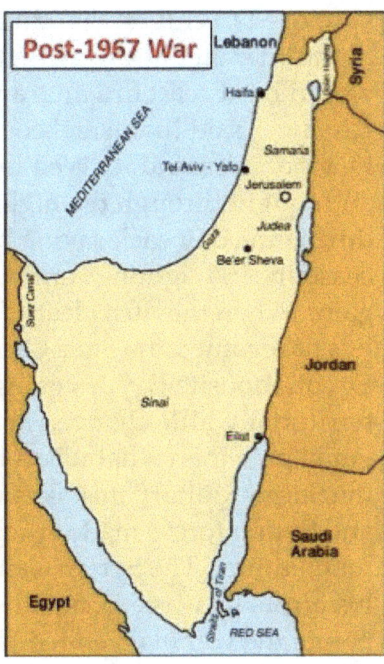

Of course this expansion of Israel did not sit well with the rest of the middle east who saw the initial land Israel was slated to be given by the UN in 1948 CE as much too much. Non-Jews in the middle east saw/see Israel as a nightmarish monster getting larger the more it fights. Yet all the other times it had fought had been on short notice before so Egypt, Syria and Jordan figured if they simply planned and coordinated ahead of time then the results would be different. So in 1973 CE Egypt, and Syria coordinated a simultaneous invasion of Israel that took place during month of Ramadan in 1973 CE which coincidentally also took place during the Jewish holiday of Yom Kippur that year. Hence this war was known as the Yom Kippur War or the Ramadan war. It lasted more than 6 days this time, 19 to be precise; from October 6th to the 25th. On October 22nd a ceasefire was brokered between the US and the USSR via the UN and the war was supposed to end on the 22nd. However since that was nighttime satellites were unable to know what the lines would be at ceasefire time and the US Secretary of State Kissinger said that Israel could fight through the night and he wouldn't mind it. Well Israel and Egypt did just that and fought through the night and then kept on fighting during the day each saying both violated the UN declared ceasefire. So fighting continued a few more days to Israel's gain. When the dust cleared Israel gained in Syria while Egypt regained the Suez Canal but Israel got parts of Egypt opposite Egypt's gains in the Sinai. So after 19 days territorially little changed and Israel actually got more land again than what it had before the war despite losing the Suez. Military mistakes were made by all but Egyptian and Syrian forces made crucial errors that stifled their momentum. The Syrian General was a Druze and due to his errors he was executed by the Syrian government before the war even ended. While it might seem pathetic on Egypt and Syria's part when this war broke out the American CIA said they expected Israel to overwhelm the Arabs in 72-96 hours, or 4 days total. So for the West it was shocking that the Arabs were able to last that long against Israel while for the middle east it was yet another military disappointment and disgrace. Yet for Israel it was a cause for fear and on October 9th, 1973 CE the Israeli Prime Minister threatened to use nuclear weapons "for defense". However today the international community largely pretends the Jewish state of Israel doesn't have any nuclear weapons even though they threatened to use them in 1973 CE. Whereas no other states in the middle east have nuclear capabilities even til today, so that the Jews have had nuclear weapons since at least 1973 shows the lopsided extent of American funding and Israel's reliance upon US taxes. In the midst of this war on October 19th, Richard Nixon passed a bill to send Israel $2.2 billion dollars in emergency military aid. So in response to this blatant excessive military aid to Israel in the middle of a war the nations of OPEC decided to reduce oil production by 5% and they stopped selling oil to America which caused gas prices in America to skyrocket as oil supply was sparse in the US for awhile. To ensure such scarcity didn't happen again, Nixon then nixxed the US dollar's tie to gold and made a deal with Saudi Arabia to create the fiat Petro-Dollar wherein the KSA would sell all its oil in US dollars. Many Muslims, Palestinians and the anti-Israel anti-Zionism crowd think this flip-flop by Saudia Arabia was a betrayal and cite it as the starting point of Saudi Arabia's treachery to the cause. Which many violent Muslim extremists, like Osama bin Laden, cite as reasons to attack the Saudi state and overthrow it. So while on paper maps the Yom Kippur war didn't result in much territorial change either way, it was a key turning point in the global economy and the rise of violent Muslim extremists. Nevertheless the map still changed after the Yom Kippur war.

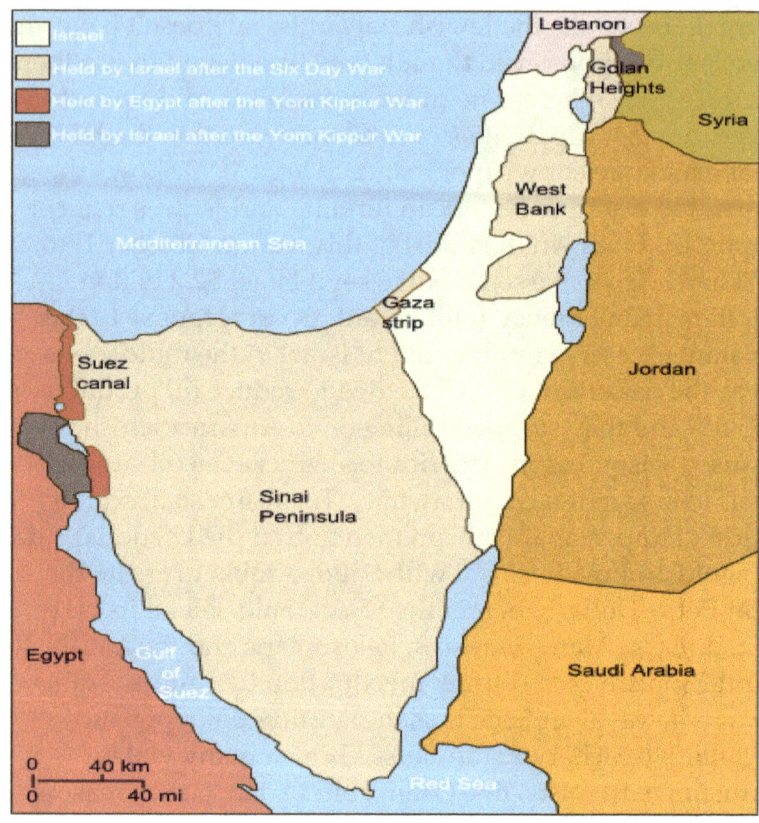

In 1974 CE Israel withdrew to more defensible positions on the Syrian Golan heights and in 1975 CE they made an agreement with Egypt exchanging territory to make the maps cleaner and get "peace talks" started in a positive direction. By 1975 due to negotiations the map looked different once again.

In September 1978 CE the Egyptian President Anwar
Sadat, the American President Jimmy Carter and the
Israeli Prime Minister Menachem Begin met at Camp
David in Maryland, USA to discuss a peace treaty. These
Camp David accords eventually led to the 1979 peace
treaty between Egypt and Israel. This treaty was highly
controversial because prior to this no Arab nation had ever
recognized Israel as a legal nation, for 32 years the middle
east unanimously said the UN did not have the authority
to create Israel and it was an illegal state. This treaty
changed that because Egypt had to recognize Israeli
borders and legally agreed to accept Israeli claims to parts

of Palestine. So while Israel lost the Sinai on the map, in legal terminology they won legitimacy from a part of the middle east thus making any future concessions of land that much more difficult and unlikely. Also the peace treaty stipulated America would give military aid to Egypt as well as Israel. And ever since then American has given billions of dollars in military aid to Egypt, on the condition of course that peace with Israel is maintained. Naturally this is military bribery where Egypt's army gets built with US taxdollars on the condition that it can't fight Israel. Americans don't like this, Egyptians don't like this but Israel loves it. This clause also allowed Muslim extremists to then denounce Egypt and say it too is an American slave following orders since it literally is in that it agrees to not fight X country in exchange for military equipment. Thus there are calls to overthrow that government and end the limits on Egyptian sovereignty but these calls for Egyptian political change are violently crushed by that military that is equipped with free American made weapons. Hence many tend to blame America for Egyptian oppression since Egypt joined Israel at the US tax trough in 1979. Yet Americans tend to never learn they are paying for both the Israeli military and the Egyptian military when they pay taxes.

At this time it seems unlikely that a peaceful solution to the problem would result in justice. This is because since the U.N.'s promise to fix the Israeli theft in 1948 CE Israel has not sat back and waited for the U.N. to take their land away. Israel has used violence to constantly expand their state taking more and more land while the U.N. continues to say they are working on a fair peaceful diplomatic solution, aka they don't want to be called anti-semitic. Yet even the original U.N. 1947 Partition Plan was unjust and criminal. Britain gave Israelis an inch, the U.N. gave them many miles, and Israel has taken an entire state and parts of other states and is still going. Violently doing all of this in the name of defense. So what should the Palestinian people do, realistically? If only one thing can be obtained, which would you choose peace or justice? If it were you and your family that was evicted from your home with all your possessions consumed by others, would you make the same choice? This is the essence of the conflict in the land of Palestine. However words don't quite show the full picture, so I included a timeline of how the demographic changed since 1946 CE to the present:

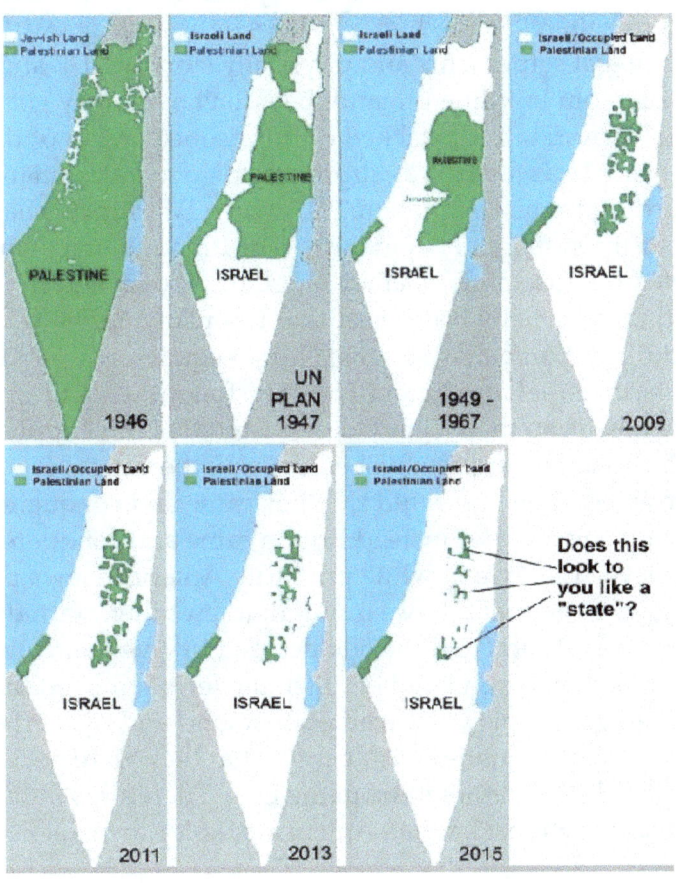

That little strip of Palestine by the sea is known as Gaza, it is 25 miles long it's width varies to 3.7 and 7.5 miles. An average person could walk the whole strip end to end in one day. It is 141 square miles and nearly 2 million people live there, meaning one person for every 2.5 square ft. The modern conflict in Palestine stems from those in Palestine saying the land the UN promised them was stolen by Israel which Israel doesn't offer in exchange for peace but just tells the people of Palestine to get out. Thus you see the green land blocks decreasing because the state of Israel with the IDF simply builds new homes for Jews in the green zone and then says it is Israel because Jews live there. And when non-Jews fight back against such illegal settlements and physically stop the IDF and Israelis from building on land they don't own, they get called terrorists and attacked or imprisoned. Most of the land Israel has today was supposed to go to Palestinians according to the UN plan in 1947 which Palestinians had forced upon them to begin with. The fundamental dispute started because of democracy and the UN plan and it continues partially because of that UN plan and the UN meddling. Some may say that "Might equals right" and that since Israel fought and Palestine fought what they have now is all they legally deserve but this can't apply here. If Israel were established the way the Crusader states were then one could say they came and conquered fair and square. But instead Britain came and conquered, then let Jews move in while primarily American Jews paid the Jews to go there, those immigrant Jews then started a violent revolution and the UN decided to give them land which no Jews even lived on, then the Jews removed the non-Jewish people who lived on that land and took other land from other non-Jewish people that they were never supposed to get as a gift from the UN. Therefore Arab nations fought back while America paid for the Israeli military and the UN insists Israel has a "right to exist" because they created it due to a vote wherein the middle east voted NO. And that too is a fundamental core issue in that *"Can the UN just vote to create a Jewish country in a holy land that doesn't belong to Jews which they didn't even live on, and where those who did live there voted no?"* Can X countries voting that Jews be given Y land to make a state be considered as having a legal right to Y land? If so then what if the Y countries vote that X land is given to Muslims and the people of X have to move to the moon or die? Obviously both options are evil and unjust, but that's democracy for you. Thus I don't think the UN will solve the problem because they made it a problem to begin with, the UN is the fundamental problem. I don't blame the Jews for trying, I blame the tools the Jews used. Instead of Israel being made the way the Crusader States were, they got made similar to how the white man made America, except the Palestinian people didn't sell their land like the Native Americans were duped/pressured into doing. So it's actually worse than the colonization of America, because the Jewish colonists play the victim card of "defense" just like how the white man played the victim card of "defense against Indian savages". However Native Americans had more reason to believe what the white man said about wanting peace, whereas publicly the Jewish proponents and the governments of Israel have said many times that Israel plans to make it's future map look like:

While in 1968 CE Christians abandoned the 1919 CE plan for Israel and drafted a new "Promised Land" they think and hope the nation of Israel will become:

So Israel can't claim to be "just trying to survive" because they actively have plans to expand for religious reasons and are currently doing so. Also what the Christians don't understand with their claims of God promising the Jews X territory is that Judaism is an evolving religion with evolving texts, Jews at this time are actively waiting for a "Messiah" to come and change the rules of their religion and conquer the world. So the notion that Jews will just stick to their peace plans and stop expanding their border is bogus. Religiously they have no limit to what they think is rightfully "Jewish land" because they still believe a new God-sent leader will come to them, and whether that leader comes or not it doesn't matter because anybody can claim they are that guy in order to justify expanding the borders and this has in fact happened throughout history. Jews have a permanent casus belli to wage war whenever they want and be right for doing so for religious reasons. There is no territorial settlement Jews can ever religiously accept because their faith is still evolving and they expect new instructions from God to come regarding their territorial borders, hence their borders truly have no limit even if Christians think otherwise. Christians can't expect a Jew to stick to an interpretation of biblical borders because to Jews their Scripture is evolutionary and still in the process of being completed. Also textually speaking there is no set border for "Israel" any who thinks there is has been mistaken. If you read the biblical books of Joshua, Judges and Kings throughout them the ancient state of Israel is fighting wars over land for religious reasons and never once do they claim that God gave them a right to that territory and that Israel is a certain latitude and longitude because God said so. The biblical Jews who fought for Israel never had a notion that there was a limit on the "Promised Land", the promised land was basically whatever they got through conquest. The Jews never ever said, "*Let's stop fighting people for territory because God only promised us X amount of land.*" This concept came up later when bible students deduced that certain tribes dwelled in certain regions and reconstructed the territory biblical Israel would have been. Yet that's just a modern extrapolation from the text, there is no promise from God that Jews deserve the land between point A , B, C and D. People have simply taken the bible and tried to use it to justify modern Jewish land grabs. Basically religious people just use the biblical text to say *"Actually the Jews should have more land than they already got/took. So rather than oppose them we should help them get even more land."* That is the fundamental thought process and motivations of Zionists who quote "Promised Land" myths. This "promise" is illusionary and was never cited by the leaders of biblical Israel because it never existed, today it's just a religious ploy to justify wicked politics and disguise the reality that there is no limit to Jewish/Zionist greed for holy land. The "Promised Land" will always be more than what they currently have. Maybe you've heard of the saying "Give em an inch and they take a mile." Well the Arab middle east gave the Zionists nothing but now they got most of Palestine. In fact in 1937 CE when the Peel Partition was proposed David Ben Gurion said the Peel Partition would be acceptable as a "first step" writing, *"This is because this increase in possession is of consequence not only in itself, but because through it we increase our strength, and every increase in strength helps in the possession of the land as a whole. The establishment of a state, even if only on a portion of the land, is the maximal reinforcement of our strength at the present time and a powerful boost to our historical endeavors to liberate the entire country."* Later in 1938 CE Ben-Gurion said *"We shall smash these frontiers which are being forced upon us, and not necessarily by war. I believe an agreememnt between us and the Arab State could be reached in a not too distant future."* He said this before WWII and before Israel ever existed, in that anything the Jewish/Zionist people got was just a crumb that would help them get more of the prized pie they ultimately plan to seize in entirety. Peace has never been a part of the Jew/Zionist agenda, they religiously desire total occupation and any "peace talk" is only done to stall or increase Israeli strength

while getting peaceful nibbles. Just like the peace talks
America had with the Native Americans. Ask them how
their peace agreements turned out, if you can find any.
Thus lies a key difference in that it's like a replay of the
white man colonization except we can see the plan before
it comes to fruition, thus we can stop it from happening; in
theory. Yet is the world trying to stop and reverse
Zionism? Gaza has been blockaded by Israel since 2007 CE
through land, air and sea. Basically if you live in Gaza,
you practically can't get anything from any other country
unless it's smuggled in or from a U.N. approved charity
organization, but since America and Israel have labeled
Gaza as a terrorist nation smuggling stuff into Gaza is
risky. In 2015 CE America sent Israel $3.7 billion dollars
explicitly for military aid, which amounts to $10.2 million
per day and America increases it's military aid to Israel
every year. Some have tried to add up all the military aid
the U.S. has sent to Israel from 1949-2015 CE and adjusting
for inflation the lowest figure that's estimated is $124.3
billion. Keep in mind all these dollars were explictly for
the Israeli military and they were all U.S. taxpayer dollars.
Thus many blame America for any and all actions done by
the Israeli military, especially when the weapons Israel
uses on Palestinians say *"Made in the U.S.A."* on them.
Israel itself had few military grade weapons until after
America became it's ally in 1948 CE and equipped the IDF,
so it's truly no stretch to give credit for most of the military
activity of Israel since 1948-Present to America. Hence in
America they teach people that Israel is good because for
America to be responsible for the military of bad guys
would mean America was not good and politically
Americans cannot be told they were bad guys since 1948
CE. But why does America fund Israel and it's military
thereby neglecting it's own needy citizens? Usually most
Americans will say because of the Jewish holocaust of

WWII, for the sake of democracy in the middle east, because of the bible, or because the people of Israel kill Muslims and they are the types that like Muslims getting killed. Or as the famous Jewish proponent of Laisse Faire Capitalism Ayn Rand said in 1974 CE, "*Further, why are the Arabs against Israel? (This is the main reason I support Israel.) The Arabs are one of the least developed cultures. They are typically nomads. Their culture is primitive, and they resent Israel because it's the sole beachhead of modern science and civilization on their continent. When you have civilized men fighting savages, you support the civilized men, no matter who they are. Israel is a mixed economy inclined toward socialism. But when it comes to the power of the mind – the development of industry in that wasted desert continent – versus savages who don't want to use their minds, then if one cares about the future of civilization, don't wait for the government to do something. Give whatever you can. This is the first time I've contributed to a public cause: helping Israel in an emergency.*" But how could she honestly think that Israel were the good guys or the underdogs in need of help to survive? This is because of the way Zionists portray the issue. Now for the sake of fairness, I will also show the map the Zionists show to entice people to side with Israel.

Israel's land concessions for peace, 1967-2011

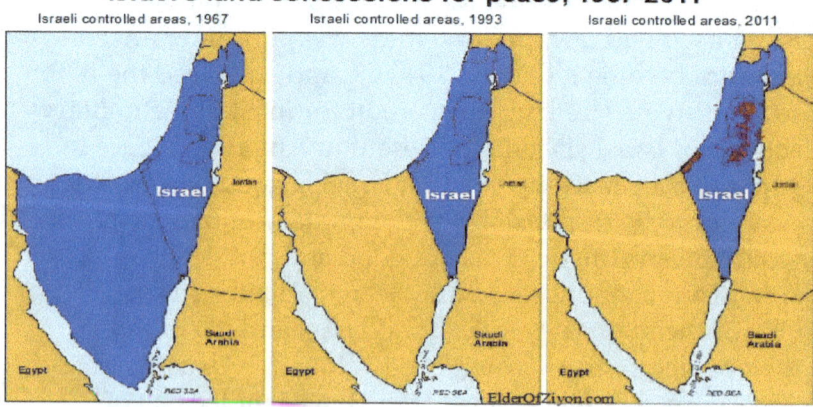

All of the land Israel gave up was in the pursuit of peace.

Regarding the Holocaust, despite all the theories against the hyperbolic Jewish extermination of 6 million during WWII, what bothers me is that people claim this is the greatest crime in human history. The greatest crime in human history is to call people to disbelieve in and disobey God, or to worship something other than or alongside God. Although if we were to focus solely on the violent human to human crimes, the native inhabitants of America were treated much worse than the Jews were during WWII. It is estimated that the European colonists exterminated 50 million people whom they referred to as savage Indians. 50 million people in the colonial era is a much larger percentage of the world's population than 6 million people were in the 1940s CE. If any ethnic group is going to be playing the pity card of world victim then it should be the Native Americans, but because they do not have the wealth, political or media influence like the various Jewish lobbies and organizations around the world people rarely consider that more than 8 times as many "Indians" were eliminated during colonization than Jews allegedly were during a World War. The "Indians" have been reduced to so few in number people forget that they even exist. People don't even realize George Washington as the first President of America ordered that entire native villages be completely destroyed with every native man, woman and child being exterminated. After America became a country the natives called George Washington "Caunotaucarius" which in their language meant "Town Destroyer" becomes he was such a butcher. But it's not just the bloodshed that gets ignored. I grew up in North Tonawanda, New York. Unbeknownst to me until I was 24 years old, Tonawanda was the place where the Native American Iroquois prophet "Handsome Lake" preached his new "Longhouse Religion" between 1800-1815 CE. A Native American actually claimed to be a prophet of God who received divine revelation in the very same region I was born and raised in. His religion was widely popular too and as President Thomas Jefferson approved of and endorsed this "Longhouse Religion" thinking it would help natives to assimilate within American society. Well the assimilation happened so thoroughly that I'd guess almost nobody living in Tonawanda or North Tonawanda today knows that it was the place a Native American prophet preached a new "Indian" religion in the 1800s CE. The Native Americans don't even live around Tonawanda anymore, it's mainly a suburban middle class "white man land" because the Native Americans have been just about completely eradicated and forgotten. Yet it used to be that from the east coasts to the west coasts, from the artic north of Canada to the southern most regions of South America was all Native American land wherein millions of people lived with hundreds of thousands of different tribes each with their own unique religions and lifestyles. Despite such prominence they were condemned to "reservations" that consistently got reduced and re-moved. It used to be that everything west of the original 13 States was an "Indian Reservation" set up by the U.S.A. which *had no plans for westward expansion, but just wanted peace*", then it was everything West of the Missisippi, then West of the Rockies then little bits in between California and America that weren't states yet. Until finally the American nations decided to just point a gun in the natives faces and say "*Either you go extinct or live where we tell you on X reservation.*" Although even then the reservations were still separate sovereign nations, but they aren't sovereign nations today and most in the Americas don't even remember they still exist or that they've been oppressed. Whereas the alleged holocaust has been so heavily promoted it seems unlikely that Jews will ever be forgotten and we are constantly told to "*never forget*". Although what ever happened to "*forgive and forget*"? The Jews abolished that practice because they want to profit from interest on debt. If your great great great grandfather got beat up by somebody would you hunt down the bully's descendants and demand an apology? If past persecution is a reason for Jewish entitlement to Palestinian land then both continents of North and South America should be donated to the Native Americans and all the current inhabitants should leave all their property behind and live on another continent starting over from scratch. If that's what the Jews get for being allegedly killed, then the Native Americans are more deserving of such lavish treatment. Oh and while we are at it why not kick the white race out of Austrailia, Asia and Africa too while making every brown-skinned person live in Africa? Seriously why should non-black people be allowed to live in Africa or non-Asians be allowed to live in Asia? That's not their "ancient homeland" shouldn't the "ancient homelands" be returned to their "ancient owners" or is that just a Jew-only rule? When we look at the issue from this perspective then we can see why the state of Israel is illegal. The U.N. reports that from 1950 -2005 CE the state of Israel has killed 24 million non-Israeli people and Israel still continues to murder to this day. Yet what is the real reason America supports Israel so devoutly, it almost seems like it's a religious alliance. Is it? Well the U.S. President Calvin Coolidge said in reference to Jews fighting in the American revoltionary war, "*The Jews themselves, of whom a considerable number were already scattered throughout the colonies, were true to the teachings of their prophets. The Jewish faith is predominantly the faith of liberty*". So it kind of is a religious alliance the U.S. ideocracy has with Jews. Regarding Zionism, the 2nd American President John Quincy Adams wrote: "*I really wish the Jews again in Judea an independent nation for, as I believe, the most enlightened men of it have participated in the amelioration of the philosophy of the age."* He wrote that in the 1700s CE when Judea was Muslim territory. Adams was friends with Mordecai Manuel Noah who in 1825 CE wanted to make Grand Island, NY an exclusively Jewish Island so they would have a land from which to depart to Israel from, when the time came. Abraham Lincoln once met the Christian Zionist, Henry Wentworth Monk, who expressed hope that Jews who were suffering oppression be emancipated *"by restoring them to their national home in Palestine."* Lincoln said this was *"a noble dream and one shared by many Americans."* Lincoln also said his chiropodist was a Jew who *"has so many times 'put me upon my feet' that I would have no objection to giving his countrymen 'a leg up.'"* Benjamin Harrison, who was the U.S. president from 1889-1893 CE called for the first international conference *"to consider the Israelite claim to Palestine as their ancient home, and to promote in any other just and proper way the alleviation of their suffering condition."* and he called for this 6 years before the World Zionist Congress had their first conference to consider the same thing. So America was internationally supporting Zionism even before there was a Zionist movement. Which is ironic when you consider what the alleged discoverer of America, Columbus, prophesied after claiming to be the Messiah. In 1952 CE, 4 years after recognizing Israel, President Harry Truman said, *"I had faith in Israel before it was established, I have faith in it now,"* ... *"I believe it has a glorious future before it – not just another sovereign nation, but as an embodiment of the great ideals of our civilization."* In the 1970s CE President Jimmy Carter stated, *"<u>The United States, has a warm and a unique relationship of friendship with Israel that is morally right. It is compatible with our deepest religious convictions, and it is right in terms of America's own strategic interests.</u> We are committed to Israel's security, prosperity, and future as a land that has so much to offer the world."* It is actually an unofficial requirement that to be the American president you have to go to Israel and pray at the "wailing wall". It's actually gotten to the point where it's overtly pathetic that the vast majority of candidates running for president in America do this when they aren't even Jewish. Clearly religion has something to do with America's alliance with Israel, whether that's the religion of Christianity, Democracy, a mix of both or something else is anybody's guess but it's certainly due to some religious doctrines. Yet George Washington's Farewell Address said *"Tis our policy to steer clear of permanent alliances with any portion of the foreign world."* While Thomas Jefferson said in his inaugural address: *"Peace, Commerce and honest friendship with all nations-entangling alliances with none."* So why then does America have a permanent alliance with the Zionist State when it's forefathers forbid such relationships? Adolf Hitler provided the answer to this question when saying, *"Any alliance whose purpose is not the intention to wage war is senseless and useless."* Politically in America since 1947 CE there has been no "anti-Israel" movement, it's all pro-Israel with the only issue being how much should the U.S. be pro-Israel and there is never a question of if. Nearly every other country in the world condemns Israel as bad guys, but because of the U.S. and the U.N. support, international democracy doesn't really make a difference in Israel's status. But all that aside, religiously from a Jewish perspective the Tanakh expressly forbids the existence of any Jewish State since the destruction of the temple in Jerusalem thousands of years ago. Jewish scholars and rabbis say that Zionists hijacked their religion and that the current state of Israel shouldn't exist because it violates the religion of Judaism and the Zionist state is diametrically opposed to Judaism. Jews who practice their religion say the state of Israel has no legitimacy and that Zionists only used Judaism to steal credibility for their materialistic desires linking zionism to Jews so opposition would be labeled as anti-semitism. Being Anti-Zionist and Anti-Israel is not anti-semitic. Even being anti-Jew isn't being anti-semitic. Semites are the descendants of Shem who was the son of Noah pbuh. Most Semites are not Jewish, and ironically most Arabs are Semites. Anti-Semitic means you hate a person's race, Anti-Jewish means you hate their religion, Anti-Zionist means you hate their politics. This is why it's so important to know what words mean before we use them. The Jewish Rabbis within Israel are against the existence of the state of Israel and get beat by the Zionist state when they publicly protest it and prove through religious texts that the Jews lost their claim to statehood and that God has forbidden a Jewish state according to Jewish Scriptures. Unfortunately some foolish Christians tell Jews otherwise. Even Martin Luther King Jr. actively supported Israel and promoted Zionism. So Jews say "destroy Israel" while zealous Christians say God will destroy any who oppose Israel and God loves Israel. Meanwhile the Zionists accept the zealous U.S. and Christians support telling everyone else this prolonged violent conflict in the holy land has nothing to do with religion at all. But it's the holy land! Everything in the holy land has to do with religion. Whatever anyone may think about the issue, we have to be honest and admit that religion is at the core of the conflict. Unfortunately the secular world is loathe to think or say there is a holy war in the holy land, and that makes it worse. One must be an idiot to think religion has nothing to do with it. Christian/U.S. Zionism has become it's own type of religion. Most of the anger over the Palestine/Israel conflict is due to many people refusing to acknowledge it as a religious war. Once it is acknowledged by all as a religious war we will be less tense and divided over it, because we will know and accept the limits of debate since religious debates are well known to end amicably without people changing their positions even when proven to be wrong. If the Palestine conflict is established as a religious conflict then we'd all be able to stop arguing over what it is and work on finding the best most just solution possible. If Muslims claim the land because of Islam and Christians claim it for Christianity and Jews for Judaism then why don't we just determine which religion is true and then decide to award the true believers the land? If the other 2 faiths refuse to accept their religion and claims as being illegitimate then they should be allowed to fight for it should they so desire. Human casualties in war may be unavoidable but honesty must not be a casualty. Out of respect for the holy land it deserves that we are all honest as to our religious motives when waging religious wars over it. To fight for religious reasons is 1 thing, to lie about your reasons for fighting is another thing that is sinful even if the cause is right. What does the future hold for the Zionist expansion in Palestine? God knows best but some of these predictions by US presidents are insightful.

John Kennedy: *"We must formulate, with both imagination and restraint, a new approach to the Middle East — not pressing our case so hard that the Arabs feel their neutrality and nationalism are threatened ... while at the same time trying to hasten the inevitable Arab acceptance of the permanence of Israel We must seek a permanent settlement among Arabs and Israelis based not on an armed truce but on mutual self-interest."*

Jimmy Carter: *"I would like to emphasize, in the strongest possible terms, that our aid for Israel is not only altruistic; indeed, our close relationship with Israel is in the moral and the strategic interest of the United States. There is a mutual relationship and there is a mutual benefit and there is a mutual commitment, which has been impressed very deeply in my mind* and also in the minds of the leaders of my Government and the Government of Israel. And I will continue to work with the leaders of Israel to strengthen even further our common commitments and our common goals. We know that in a time of crisis, we can count on Israel. And the people of Israel know that in a time of crisis, they can count on the United States ... Let me assure you that in this negotiation, as we work for the legitimate rights of the Palestinians, recognized in the Camp David accords by Prime Minister Begin and President Sadat, that we will countenance no action which could hurt Israel's security. This is because of our commitment to Israel's security and well-being, and it's because Israel's security is so closely linked to the security of the United States of America ... I am opposed to an independent Palestinian state, because in my own judgement and in the judgement of many leaders in the Middle East, including Arab leaders, this would be a destabilizing factor in the Middle East and would certainly not serve the United States interests."

John Kennedy: "Quite apart from the values and hopes which the State of Israel enshrines — and the past injuries which it redeems — it twists reality to suggest that it is the democratic tendency of Israel which has interjected discord and dissension into the Near East. Even by the coldest calculations, the removal of Israel would not alter the basic crisis in the area. For, if there is any lesson which the melancholy events of the last two years and more taught us, it is that, though Arab states are generally united in opposition to Israel, their political unities do not rise above this negative position. The basic rivalries within the Arab world, the quarrels over boundaries, the tensions involved in lifting their economies from stagnation, the cross pressures of nationalism — all of these factors would still be there, even if there were no Israel."